OXFORD BOOKWORMS LIBRARY

Factfiles

Great Crimes

Stage 4 (1400 headwords)

Factfiles Series Editor: Christine Lindop

JOHN ESCOTT

Great Crimes

OXFORD UNIVERSITY PRESS

OXFORD
UNIVERSITY PRESS

Great Clarendon Street, Oxford OX2 6DP

Oxford University Press is a department of the University of Oxford.
It furthers the University's objective of excellence in research, scholarship,
and education by publishing worldwide in

Oxford New York

Auckland Cape Town Dar es Salaam Hong Kong Karachi
Kuala Lumpur Madrid Melbourne Mexico City Nairobi
New Delhi Shanghai Taipei Toronto

With offices in

Argentina Austria Brazil Chile Czech Republic France Greece
Guatemala Hungary Italy Japan Poland Portugal Singapore
South Korea Switzerland Thailand Turkey Ukraine Vietnam

ISBN: 978 0 19 423394 1

A complete recording of *Great Crimes*
is available.

Printed in China

Word count (main text): 15747

For more information on the Oxford Bookworms Library,
visit www.oup.com/elt/gradedreaders

ACKNOWLEDGEMENTS
The publishers would like to thank the following for permission to reproduce images:
Action Plus p47 (Shergar/Leo Mason); Alamy Images pp1 (Dr Crippen/Popperfoto), 32 (Lee
Harvey Oswald/Popperfoto); Corbis pp8 (Dr Crippen trial/Bettmann), 14 (Vincenzo Perugia/
Bettmann), 15 (Charles & Anne Lindbergh/Bettmann), 18 (wanted poster/Bettmann), 20
(Bruno Hauptmann/Bettmann), 23 (Great Train Robbery 1963/Bettmann), 28 (Ronald Biggs/
Greg Newton/Reuters), 30 (Kennedy shooting/Bettmann), 39 (SLA shoot-out/Bettmann),
61 (Nick Leeson/Polak Matthew/Sygma), 64 (Nick Leeson/Paul McErlane/Reuters), 66 & 68
(Charles Ponzi images/Bettmann), 69 (Sunflowers by Vincent van Gogh/National Gallery
Collection; By kind permission of the Trustees of the National Gallery, London), 56 (Ivy
"Buck" Barrow/Bettmann); Getty Images pp5 (Ethel Le Neve/Hulton Archive), 35 (Patty
Hearst/Hulton Archive), 37 (Patty Hearst/Hulton Archive), 43 (dingo/Theo Allofs/Photonica),
45 (Lindy Chamberlain/Patrick Riviere), 49 (Shergar/Hulton Archive), 51 (Bonnie & Clyde/
Hulton Archive, 55 Clyde Barrow/Hulton Archive, Bonnie Parker/Hulton Archive), 72
(Elmyr de Hory/Pierre Boulat//Time Life Pictures); Newspix pp40 (Lindy Chamberlain), 42
(Uluru search/Denis Barrett); PA Photos pp26 (Great Train Robbers/AP), 59 (Bonnie & Clyde
car/AP), 63 (DPA0).

This book is printed on paper from certified and well-managed sources.

CONTENTS

1 Dr Crippen

'I've fallen in love with one woman – but I'm already married to another. What can I do?' Thousands of men have asked themselves this question. Most of them find an answer that leaves all three people alive, but Hawley Crippen did not. So when Crippen left Europe with his young lover in 1910, an English policeman went after them, and readers of English newspapers followed the chase with excitement. It was the first chase of its kind anywhere in the world.

Dr Crippen

The story began in New York in July 1892, when Dr Hawley Harvey Crippen met Cora Turner. He was thirty years old, and was working in a hospital, and she was nineteen. Crippen immediately fell in love with Cora, and six months later they were married.

At first they continued to live in New York, and Crippen joined a company which sold medicines. This was Cora's idea. She wanted her husband to earn more money than the hospital was paying him.

Cora loved the theatre and wanted to be a singer, so her

husband paid for her to have singing lessons. Her voice was not really good enough, and she wasn't very successful. Later, when the couple moved to London, she began to sing in theatres, using the name 'Belle Elmore', but she was never famous.

Crippen was not allowed to work as a doctor in England because he had trained in America, so he continued to work for the American medicine company, and opened a London office for them.

In 1905, the Crippens moved to a house at 39 Hilldrop Crescent. They were not happy together, however. Cora was a cruel, violent woman, and the couple were always arguing, often because Cora spent more money than they could afford. She also liked to spend time with other men.

In 1907, Crippen fell in love with his secretary, a sweet, quiet girl called Ethel Le Neve. Ethel wanted him to leave his wife and marry her, but Crippen was unwilling to do this.

Then, in December 1909, Cora discovered that her husband and Ethel Le Neve were lovers. She warned Crippen that she would leave him, and take most of his money with her.

On 31 January 1910, two of Cora's theatre friends, Paul and Clara Martinetti, came to dinner with the Crippens, and during the evening Cora and her husband argued violently. The Martinettis left early. It was that night, after the Martinettis had left, that Crippen decided to kill Cora. He was tired of all the arguments and Cora's liking for other men.

The next week, Crippen told neighbours and friends that Cora had gone to America to look after someone who was sick. This came as a surprise; Cora had said nothing to them about a sick friend, or about travelling to America. Then, some weeks later, Crippen sold several of Cora's rings, and in March Ethel Le Neve moved into 39 Hilldrop Crescent to live with Crippen. He told neighbours that Cora was her aunt.

Later, when Crippen told the Martinettis and other friends of Cora's that she had become ill and had died in America, they suspected that he was lying. Finally, one of the friends went to the police with the story.

Chief Inspector Walter Dew of Scotland Yard, England's most famous police station, visited Crippen soon after this on 8 July. Walter Dew was one of the policemen who had worked on the famous Jack the Ripper murders in 1888, when five women were murdered in Whitechapel in the east of London. (The Ripper was never caught.)

Dew talked with the doctor and Ethel Le Neve. Crippen spoke calmly and confidently about his wife, making no secret of the fact that Ethel Le Neve had been his lover for several years. He also agreed that the story about his wife's death had been a lie. The truth was, he told the detective, that Cora had gone to America to live with a lover, Bruce Miller. Crippen had not wanted to tell anyone that his wife had left him, so he pretended that she had died. Inspector Dew was not completely happy with this story, but he was not able to prove that Crippen was lying. When he asked Crippen if he could search the house, Crippen agreed immediately. But Dew found nothing in the house to make him believe that anything was wrong. He even helped Crippen to prepare a small notice to go in some American newspapers, asking for news of Cora.

But Crippen was not as confident as he pretended to be. The visit from Inspector Dew had worried him, and after the detective left, he told Ethel Le Neve that they must go away and make a new life for themselves in another country.

They began by getting a boat to the Netherlands, and then went on to Brussels, in Belgium, where they moved into a hotel for several days.

When Inspector Dew visited Crippen's office on Monday 11 July, he was surprised to find that Crippen had gone. He also learned that Crippen had asked someone in the office to buy some boy's clothes. Immediately, he gave orders for another search of the house at Hilldrop Crescent. This time it did not take his men long to find part of a woman's body under the house (there was no head, and no arms or legs).

On 15 July, Crippen read in a Belgian newspaper that part of a human body had been found under the house at 39 Hilldrop Crescent. He quickly got tickets to sail on a ship – the *Montrose* – which was going to Quebec in Canada. Ethel Le Neve cut her hair short and dressed as a sixteen-year-old boy, pretending to be Crippen's son. They used the name 'Robinson'.

The ship sailed for Canada on Wednesday 20 July, but the captain of the *Montrose*, Henry Kendall, had read about Dr Crippen in the newspapers. He looked at the photographs of Crippen and Ethel Le Neve, and began to suspect that Mr Robinson and his 'son' were not what they seemed. He watched them walking around the ship. Sometimes the two 'men' held hands, he noticed. Crippen wore glasses and had a moustache; 'Mr Robinson' did not wear glasses, but he had a mark on his nose from wearing them, and he had cut off his moustache recently. The captain felt more and more certain that Mr Robinson and his son were in fact Crippen and Ethel.

But the captain had to decide quickly what to do. The *Montrose* was one of the very few Canadian Pacific ships to have a radio, but it would soon be too far from land to send a message, though it could receive them. On the afternoon of Friday 22 July, Kendall sent a radio message about his two passengers to England, and the message was passed to Inspector Dew. There was just enough time for Dew to take the night train to Liverpool and board the *Laurentic*, which left the following day for Quebec. The *Montrose* was three days ahead of the *Laurentic*, but was still eleven days from Quebec, and the *Laurentic* was a faster ship.

Ethel Le Neve dressed as a boy

On Sunday 24 July a message arrived on the *Montrose* from a London newspaper. One of their reporters was travelling on the ship. 'Are passengers excited over the chase?' the message asked. Then Captain Kendall knew that Inspector Dew had received his message. The English newspapers quickly heard what was happening and for the next week they reported the chase across the sea for their readers. It was the first time that radios were ever used to chase a criminal, and it made exciting reading. 'Is it Crippen?' 'Crippen Found' and 'A Race Across the Ocean' were some of the headlines. On board the *Montrose*, Captain Kendall made sure that none of the passengers knew anything about the chase.

On 29 July the *Laurentic* passed the *Montrose*, and soon afterwards Inspector Dew left the ship and made his plans to arrest Crippen and Ethel. Captain Kendall suggested that Inspector Dew should come onto the ship dressed as a ship's officer; the captain knew that Crippen had a gun, and he wanted the inspector to arrest Crippen before he had time to do anything dangerous.

On the morning of Sunday 31 July, Inspector Dew and a Canadian policeman left Father Point, Quebec, in a small boat. They boarded the *Montrose* and came face to face with Crippen. 'Good afternoon, Dr Crippen,' Dew said. 'Remember me? I'm Inspector Dew from Scotland Yard.' Crippen stared at the inspector for a moment or two, then said, 'Thank God it's over.' Ethel was arrested in her room, where she was found reading a book. And then reporters from the world's newspapers were allowed onto the ship.

Dew left Quebec with Crippen and Ethel the next day, and took them back to London. Dr Crippen's trial, which began on 18 October, took just three days. The jury heard how he had first poisoned his wife, then cut up her body and

THE WESTERN UNION TELEGRAPH COMPANY.
THE LARGEST TELEGRAPHIC SYSTEM IN EXISTENCE.

DIRECT ROUTE *FOR ALL PARTS OF THE* UNITED STATES.
CANADA, CENTRAL AMERICA, WEST INDIES,
SOUTH AMERICA, & *VIA THE* PACIFIC CABLE *TO* AUSTRALIA.
NEW ZEALAND, FANNING, FIJI *AND* NORFOLK ISLANDS.

ATLANTIC CABLES direct to CANADA and to NEW YORK CITY.
DIRECT WIRES TO ALL THE PRINCIPAL CITIES.

Montrose

Handcuffs Ldn Eng

To

Crippen and leneve
arrested wire later
Dew

The public are requested to hand in their replies at the Company's Stations, where free
receipts are given for the amounts charged.
CABLE ADDRESSES ARE REGISTERED FREE OF CHARGE.
No inquiry respecting this Message can be attended to without the production of this Paper.

Inspector Dew's
message after the arrest

buried it under his house. No one was surprised when they found him guilty of murder.

Ethel Le Neve was tried as an accessory – someone involved in the crime although not there when it happened – but she was found not guilty.

Dr Hawley Harvey Crippen was hanged on the morning of Wednesday 23 November 1910, in Pentonville Prison. On the same day Ethel Le Neve, dressed in black, sailed from London for New York. She lived for some time in America, but later came back to England using the name Ethel Nelson.

Dr Crippen and Ethel Le Neve in court

Later, she married Stanley Smith and the couple had two children – a son and a daughter. Smith never knew about Ethel's earlier life. She died in 1967 at the age of 85.

Walter Dew left the police a few months after he arrested Crippen, and became a private detective. He died in 1947.

In 1914 Captain Kendall was on board the ship *Empress of Ireland* when it went down off Father Point, Quebec – in exactly the same place where Crippen and Ethel were arrested. More than a thousand people died, but Kendall survived the accident.

Kendall always remembered a moment on the *Montrose* when he and Crippen were talking. They could hear the noise from the ship's radio, sending and receiving messages. 'What a wonderful thing radio is!' said Dr Crippen. But that wonderful thing meant death for Dr Crippen.

2 The *Mona Lisa* – lost and found

At 7.00 a.m. on Monday 21 August 1911, three cleaners were walking through the Salon Carré, one of the rooms in the Louvre Museum in Paris. The three men stopped to look at one of the world's most famous paintings – the *Mona Lisa*.

'This is the most valuable picture in the world,' said one of the men. 'They say it's worth one and a half million francs.'

After staring at the famous smile for a moment or two, the three men then walked on to the Grand Gallery, which was the next room, to continue with some repair work. It was 8.35 a.m. before they passed through the Salon Carré again, and one of the men noticed that the *Mona Lisa* had now gone.

'They've taken it away,' he laughed. 'They're afraid we'll steal it!'

The Louvre

The *Mona Lisa*

The other men laughed with him, and went back to their work. It was not unusual for someone to move a painting in the gallery. Paintings were often taken away, photographed, and then put back later, so the three cleaners did not think any more about it.

At 7.20 the next morning, Poupardin, one of the Louvre guards, passed through the Salon Carré and noticed that the *Mona Lisa* was not in its place. He too thought that someone had taken it away to photograph it.

At nine o'clock a painter called Louis Béroud arrived at the museum. He was painting a picture of the Salon Carré, and he was annoyed to see that the *Mona Lisa* was not there.

'Where is the *Mona Lisa*?' he asked Poupardin.

'It's gone to be photographed,' replied the guard.

Béroud decided to wait for the return of the famous painting, but by early afternoon he had had enough. He told Poupardin to go and ask the photographer to send back the painting. 'I don't have much more time,' he said.

Poupardin went away – and came back quickly.

'The picture isn't there!' he said excitedly. 'They don't know anything about it!' And he hurried away to find his boss.

At three o'clock that afternoon, people were asked to leave the Louvre. 'The museum is closing,' they were told. But it was only when they read the newspapers the next day that they discovered the reason. Someone had stolen the *Mona Lisa*!

The museum was closed for a week. Police believed that the famous painting could be hidden somewhere in the building, and they began to search. They also took the fingerprints of everyone who worked at the museum.

Then the police found the empty frame from the *Mona Lisa* on some back stairs. Slowly, they began to put together the story of what had happened.

The thief came to the museum on Sunday 20 August and hid in the building after the galleries closed. At 7.30 the next morning he took the *Mona Lisa*, then went into another room and down the stairs where the police later found the frame. He stopped to take the painting out of the frame, then went on to a door which led into a courtyard. The door was locked so he had to take off the doorknob in order to break the door open. He had only managed to take off the doorknob when he heard a noise, so he pushed the doorknob into his pocket, and sat on the stairs. A man who worked for the museum walked by. He said later that he thought the man on the stairs was one of the museum cleaners, and he unlocked and opened the door for him.

The thief went out into the courtyard, walked across it and opened an unlocked door that led into the street. He ran off towards the Pont du Carrousel, throwing the doorknob away as he ran. It was found later by the police.

When the Louvre opened again, crowds hurried to look at the empty place on the wall of the Salon Carré. They could not believe their eyes. The *Mona Lisa* really *had* been stolen!

Police questioned hundreds of people, searched hundreds of houses, flats and rooms, took fingerprints, and talked to other criminals. They also found a thumbprint on the glass in the empty picture frame.

But they did not find the *Mona Lisa*. As time went on, the people of France began to believe that they would never see the famous picture again.

In autumn 1913 a man called Alfredo Geri, who bought and sold paintings, put a notice in several Italian newspapers, saying that he was interested in buying works of art of all kinds. In November that year a letter arrived at his office in Florence, in Italy. The writer, who signed his name as 'Leonard', said that he was an Italian living in Paris. He said that he had stolen the *Mona Lisa* and wanted to return it to Italy.

At first Geri thought the letter was probably from a madman, but to be sure he showed it to his friend Giovanni Poggi at the Uffizi Gallery in Florence. They decided to write to Leonard and ask him to bring the painting to Milan.

On Wednesday 10 December, a thin young man with a small dark moustache arrived at Geri's office. He told Geri that the *Mona Lisa* was in his hotel room, and that he wanted 500,000 lire (100,000 dollars) for the picture. He said that Napoleon had stolen the painting from Italy, and he wanted it to come back to the country where it belonged. (In fact, although Napoleon did take a lot of paintings from Italy in the nineteenth century, the *Mona Lisa* was not one of them.)

The next day, Geri and Poggi went to the young man's room in the Hotel Tripoli-Italia – and there was the famous painting. Poggi asked if he could take it to the Uffizi Gallery and look at it together with photographs of the real *Mona Lisa*. The young man agreed, and the three of them went to the gallery.

Later, the young man went back to his hotel – and was arrested by Italian detectives.

The young thief's real name was Vincenzo Perugia, and he was a house painter. He had worked for a short time at the museum, and the police had in fact questioned him soon after the painting was stolen. They had searched his room at the time, but had found nothing.

Perugia had been in trouble with the police before. But his fingerprints, kept by the police, only showed his *right* thumb, and the thumbprint from the glass in the empty frame had been a print of the *left* thumb.

Perugia's photos and fingerprints

Now the police searched his room in Paris once more, and this time they found a diary with a list of the names of people who bought and sold paintings in America, Germany, and Italy.

They also questioned two other Italian house painters who were suspected of hiding the picture when Perugia's room was first searched. Finally they had to let them go.

The trial of Vincenzo Perugia began on 4 June 1914 in Florence. When questioned, this is what he told the judge:

'I entered the Louvre about seven o'clock in the morning. I was able to get into the Salon Carré. I took the *Mona Lisa*, took it out of its frame, then left.'

'How did you leave?' asked the judge.

'The same way I came in,' answered Perugia.

He was sent to prison for one year and fifteen days, but this was later shortened to seven months.

Some people believe that Perugia was working with other criminals, one of whom was a painter, and that they offered the missing *Mona Lisa* to rich Americans. Each of the American collectors bought their *Mona Lisa* secretly, not realizing that it was one of a number of forged copies. Could this be true? We will probably never know.

3 The Lindbergh kidnapping

It was the evening of Tuesday 1 March 1932. Charles and Anne Lindbergh finished dinner at their large country house near the village of Hopewell in New Jersey, USA, and Charles Lindbergh went to work in his library. Soon after 9.00 p.m., he heard a noise like something breaking, but it was a stormy night and he thought it was probably thunder. His wife heard nothing. Upstairs their son Charles Junior (often called 'Little It') was asleep in his bed.

Charles and Anne Lindbergh

Just after 10.00 p.m., Betty Gow, the child's nurse, went to check that Charles Junior was all right. She found the little bed empty. Quickly, she went to find Mrs Lindbergh, but the boy was with neither his mother nor his father.

In the child's bedroom, the window was open, and there was rainwater and dirt on the floor. There was also an envelope near the window.

Lindbergh called the police, and they hurried to the house. Detectives found a rough wooden ladder about twenty-five metres from the window of the child's bedroom, and two footprints in the garden. The top step of the ladder was broken – and Charles Lindbergh remembered the noise he had heard earlier. A detective checked the envelope for fingerprints but found none. Inside the envelope there was a note in poor English:

dear Sir!

Have 50 000 $ redy 25 000 $ in 20 $ bills 15 000
$ in 10 $ bills and 10 000 $ in 5 $ bills. After
2–4 days we will inform you were to deliver the
Mony.

We warn you for making anyding public or for
notify the Police. the child is in gute care.

Indication for all letters are

signature

and 3 holes.

The Lindberghs were very rich and famous people. Charles Lindbergh was the first man to fly a plane alone across the Atlantic; in 1927 he had flown from New York to Paris in 33½ hours. His wife Anne was the daughter of Dwight Morrow, one of the richest bankers in the east of America.

And now their son had been kidnapped.

Soon people all over America heard the news on the radio or read it in their newspapers. President Hoover promised to do everything possible to make sure that the child was found.

Usually the Lindberghs only went to their Hopewell home at weekends. Normally they spent the rest of the week with Anne Lindbergh's family in Englewood, which was nearer to New York. But Charles Junior had caught a cold and Mrs Lindbergh wanted him to stay at Hopewell until he was better. So how did the kidnappers know that the Lindberghs were there that Tuesday evening? It was one of the first questions detectives asked.

People working for the Lindberghs were immediately suspected of having a part in the kidnapping. The child's nurse, Betty Gow, was questioned carefully but the police finally let her go. Another woman working at the Lindbergh house, 28-year-old Violet Sharpe, first told the police that she was at the cinema on the night of the kidnapping. Later she changed her story and said that she had been with a man. In May she changed her story again. On 10 June, when she heard that the police wanted to question her once more, she killed herself.

Lindbergh told the newspapers that he would not try to harm the kidnappers if they returned the boy safely. He then hired two criminals to try and contact the kidnappers. Lindbergh offered a reward of 50,000 dollars for the return of his son. This is worth more than a million dollars in today's money.

Before Lindbergh's helpers could do anything, however, the kidnappers made contact with Dr John Francis Condon.

He was a 72-year-old teacher who often wrote letters to the *Bronx Home News*, a New York newspaper. He was told to take Lindbergh's money to the Woodlawn Cemetery in the Bronx. A meeting time was arranged over the telephone, and Condon went to the cemetery.

A man who looked Italian walked by with something across half his face. Condon guessed that the man was checking to see if there were any police around. Then Condon saw a second man standing in the shadows, with his hat pulled down over his face and something covering his mouth. When the second man spoke, Condon recognized the voice. It was the man who had spoken to him on the telephone. He was about thirty-five years old and had brown hair. He said his name was John and that there were six people in the gang, two of them women.

He told Condon that the child was well, but then asked, 'Would I burn if the baby was dead? Would I burn if I did not kill it?' By 'would I burn' he meant would he die in the electric chair – the punishment used in America at that time for kidnappers and murderers. Condon saw the danger at once. The answer to both questions was yes – so there was no reason for the kidnappers to keep the child alive.

Condon and the man made more arrangements to contact each other, then 'Cemetery John' (as he became known) disappeared into the night.

Several more messages were passed between the two men, and then Condon received a package in the post. Inside were Charles Lindbergh Junior's sleeping suit, and a note about the money for the kidnappers.

At 7.45 p.m. on Saturday 2 April 1932, Condon and Lindbergh went to St Raymond's Cemetery in the Bronx. Lindbergh waited in the car while Condon went into the cemetery. They both heard a voice shout: 'Hey, Doc!'

Soon afterwards, Cemetery John appeared, with his hat pulled down over his face. 'I have 50,000 dollars,' said Condon. The man gave him a note. It said that the boy was on a boat called *Nelly*, near the Elizabeth Islands, off the coast of Massachusetts. Lindbergh searched for several days, but he never found the boat.

Then, on 12 May, two lorry drivers found the body of Charles Lindbergh Junior in some woods about seven kilometres from the Lindbergh's Hopewell house. He had died only a few hours after the kidnapping on 1 March.

More than two years passed. The police knew the numbers on the dollar bills which Condon had given to the kidnappers, and they asked people who worked in shops to watch for them. But it was 16 September 1934 before detectives caught a 34-year-old German, Bruno Richard Hauptmann, when he paid for petrol with a ten-dollar bill – one of the bills that were given to Cemetery John. When Hauptmann was arrested, police found another of the bills in his pocket. And at his home they discovered another 13,760 dollars of Lindbergh's money. They also learned that Hauptmann was a carpenter, whose job it was to make things from wood – like ladders.

Hauptmann said that the money belonged to a business friend, Isidor Fisch, who had gone back to Germany and died there in March 1934. Hauptmann said Fisch had left the money behind when he went to Germany. And because Fisch had owed Hauptmann about 7,500 dollars, Hauptmann had taken it.

'I had no part in the kidnapping,' Hauptmann told detectives, 'and I did not write the notes to Lindbergh.'

But the police refused to believe him, and they said that

Hauptmann in court

the writing on the notes was the same as Hauptmann's.

At the trial in January 1935, Charles Lindbergh said that he recognized Hauptmann's voice. He also changed his story. He now said that Cemetery John had called 'Hey, Doctor!' and not 'Hey, Doc!', and that he had spoken with a foreign accent. Dr Condon told a different story too. When he was first questioned by police, he had said that he was not sure whether Hauptmann was Cemetery John. At the trial, however, he said that he was now sure that Hauptmann was the man that he had spoken to in the cemetery. The jury believed both men.

Hauptmann said that he had been working in New York at the time of the kidnapping. His wife and employer both agreed with this (although his employer would not speak at the trial), but the papers to prove it could not be found.

The jury finally decided that Bruno Hauptmann was guilty of kidnapping and murder, and he died in the electric chair at Trenton State Prison, New Jersey, on 3 April 1936. But questions are still asked about the trial.

Was the writing on the kidnap notes *really* the same as Bruno Hauptmann's?

How did Hauptmann know that Charles Lindbergh and his family were at the house near Hopewell on that stormy night in March 1932? He told the police that he had never been to the village of Hopewell, and that he did not know it.

Was the baby found in the woods the Lindbergh baby? One report said that this body was 10 cm taller than Charles Junior.

What happened to the rest of the money?

Why did Violet Sharpe kill herself?

After all these years, the Lindbergh kidnapping remains a mystery.

4 The Great Train Robbery

In the early hours of 8 August 1963, the night mail train from Glasgow to London's King's Cross station was making good time. To the driver, 58-year-old Jack Mills, and the fireman, 26-year-old David Whitby, it seemed just like a normal night. But they would remember this night for the rest of their lives.

Nearly all the train's twelve coaches were used as offices for the Royal Mail. Letters and packets were put into groups for different towns and cities. One special coach – for valuable packets – was carrying 128 bags. Many of them contained old banknotes which were going to be destroyed.

At 3.03 a.m., almost 80 kilometres from London and near the small village of Cheddington, Jack Mills suddenly saw a red signal. He immediately brought his engine to a stop. It was unusual to find a red signal here, so David Whitby got out of the engine to walk to the emergency telephone, which was behind a signal box. But two men in black balaclavas (later known to be Buster Edwards and Bob Welch) came out of the darkness and pushed him down on the ground at the side of the railway. One man told Whitby, 'If you shout, I'll kill you!'

Two men climbed into the engine and Jack Mills tried to fight them. One of the men hit Mills over the head. Meanwhile, others in the gang quietly and efficiently unfastened the ten coaches at the back of the train, leaving just the front two fastened to the engine. The valuable packets coach was the second of these.

Bridego Bridge

David Whitby was brought back and the robbers made Jack Mills drive the train very slowly to Bridego Bridge, 600 metres away. The other ten coaches were left behind, and the seventy people inside them did not realize what was happening.

Other gang members wearing balaclavas were waiting at the bridge with Land Rovers and a lorry. They had tied something white to a stick by the railway to mark the place where they wanted the engine to stop.

They broke the windows of the valuable packets coach and made the Post Office workers lie down on the floor. Next, the robbers passed bags of old banknotes out into the darkness. The bags were passed from one person to the next until they arrived at the lorry. When 120 bags had been put on the lorry, it was time to leave. The lorry was full, and the sky was beginning to get light. The train robbers put handcuffs on Mills and Whitby and warned them not to try to escape for at least half an hour. Then they disappeared into the night. The whole robbery – from stopping the train to leaving with the bags – had taken just forty minutes.

The 120 bags contained 2.5 million pounds in old notes. Today, that would be about 25 million pounds, and at the time it was the biggest robbery ever. The newspapers were soon calling it the 'crime of the century', and the Post Office quickly offered 10,000 pounds for information that would lead to the arrest of the robbers.

One of the first things that detectives wanted to know was how the robbers had changed the railway signal from 'Go' to 'Stop'. They soon had the answer. The robbers had covered the green 'Go' signal with a glove, then used their own red light which they had brought with them.

And where were the robbers now?

Weeks before, the gang had bought an old farmhouse – called Leatherslade Farm – about 50 kilometres from the bridge. They had waited there before the robbery, drinking beer and playing cards, and they went there afterwards to count their money. About fifteen men were involved in the robbery, and each man would get more than 150,000 pounds.

They had planned to stay at the farmhouse for several days, but during the afternoon of Thursday 8 August they heard something on the radio news that made them change their plans. The police said that they were sure the gang were hiding not more than 50 kilometres from Bridego Bridge. In fact the police were only guessing this. The gang had told

Leatherslade Farm

Mills and Whitby to wait for thirty minutes before getting help, so the gang's hiding place was probably thirty minutes – or 50 kilometres – from the bridge.

The gang left Leatherslade Farm on Friday 9 August. They had paid another man a lot of money to clean the farmhouse after they had gone, but he took the money and did nothing. By the following Monday the police had found the farmhouse. Inside there were empty Post Office bags – and bottles and playing cards covered in fingerprints. Soon the police knew that among the people in the gang there were several well-known criminals – Bruce Reynolds, Buster Edwards, Ronnie Biggs, Bob Welch, Roy James, John Daly, and Charlie Wilson. Now they had the job of finding them.

Roger Cordrey, who had fixed the railway signal to show red instead of green, and Bill Boal, another of the robbers,

Bruce Reynolds
Charlie Wilson

Jimmy White
Ronald "Buster" Edwards

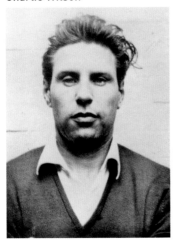

tried to find a garage for their van in Bournemouth. But they picked the wrong person to ask. The owner of the garage was the wife of a policeman who had died, and she immediately suspected something when the robbers paid her from a thick packet of banknotes. She phoned the police while the two men were putting their van into the garage. The police caught them and found 78,892 pounds in the van. Later they found more money in suitcases hidden in a wood.

By the end of the year most of the gang had been caught.

Charlie Wilson was arrested without any trouble at his Clapham home in South London. Roy James was more difficult to catch. He was hiding in a house in St John's Wood in North London. But when he saw the police, James took a bag containing 12,000 pounds and climbed up on to the roof to try and escape. He jumped and ran along neighbours' roofs, but more than forty policemen were in the surrounding streets and James finally jumped down into the waiting arms of one of them. John Daly was arrested the same day. But Buster Edwards, Bruce Reynolds, and Jimmy White were still missing. And so was two million pounds.

The trial of the robbers began on 24 January 1964, at Aylesbury in Buckinghamshire. The police did not want the trial to take place at the Old Bailey – the famous London criminal court – because they were afraid that powerful London criminals would try to frighten people on the jury.

All the robbers were tried together, and they all said they were not guilty except Roger Cordrey. The trial took two months. Neither Jack Mills nor David Whitby could be sure which men had worn the balaclavas, and nobody had seen the robbers at the farm. But the lawyers brought in 200 witnesses, the judge took six days to talk to the jury, and the jury took two days to decide that all the robbers except John Daly were guilty. The guilty men were sent to prison for up to thirty years.

Jimmy White was finally caught in Dover on the south coast of England. Police suspected that he was trying to travel abroad. Buster Edwards gave himself up in 1966. He had been living in Mexico. And Bruce Reynolds, the leader of the gang, was finally caught in 1968. He was arrested in Torquay, in Devon, and was sent to prison for twenty-five years.

But two of the gang did not stay in prison for long.

In August 1964, Charlie Wilson escaped from Birmingham's Winson Green prison when three men broke into the prison to get him out. He went to France and Mexico, but was finally caught again in Canada, and went to prison in 1968. After he finished his time in prison he went to live in Spain, where he was murdered by a gunman in 1990.

In July 1965, Ronnie Biggs got out of Wandsworth prison with three other prisoners while they were walking between the prison buildings. The four men climbed the 6-metre prison wall using a rope ladder, which had been thrown down by an 'escape gang' outside.

Biggs finally went to live in Brazil, after first escaping to Spain and then Australia. He lived in Rio de Janeiro for

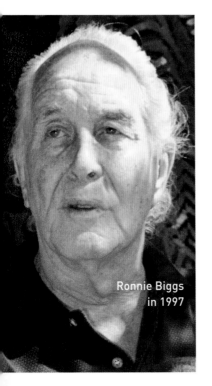

Ronnie Biggs in 1997

many years with his girlfriend, Raimunda Castro, and their son Michael. In May 2001 Biggs, now seventy-one years old and in poor health, decided to return to England. He was immediately arrested and sent to Belmarsh Prison to finish the rest of his thirty years in prison.

In 1993, Biggs said that four gang members were never caught. Nobody, other than the robbers and possibly a few other criminals, knows who they are. But perhaps they know what happened to the missing 2 million pounds.

5 The Kennedy assassination

'Where were you when you heard that President Kennedy had been shot?'

Many people who were alive at the time can answer this question. It is a moment that they can remember clearly, because the news was so shocking and so unexpected.

On the morning of 22 November 1963 John F. Kennedy

The president's car in Dallas

and his wife Jacqueline arrived in Dallas, Texas. At 11.50 a.m. a line of seven cars left the airport at Love Field. At the back of the second car were the President of the United States of America and his wife; in front of them were John Connally, Governor of Texas, and his wife Nellie. Excited crowds stood along the streets of Dallas, enjoying the sunny weather and watching for the car with the open top in which the president and his wife were travelling. They waved and shouted their good wishes as the president's car passed.

'You can't say Dallas doesn't love you,' Mrs Connally told the Kennedys, as they listened to the shouts and saw the smiling faces.

Millions of Americans were watching on television as

Moments after the shots

the cars turned slowly from Houston Street into Elm Street at 12.30. One of the buildings with a view over Elm Street was the Texas Book Depository, a large building where schoolbooks were kept.

President Kennedy was waving at the crowds when there was the sound of a gun shot. The president's hand stopped moving and then, as a second shot was heard, his hand went to his neck. There was a third shot (and perhaps a fourth), and his head was suddenly covered in blood. John Connally, who had also been hit in the back by a bullet, fell to the floor of the car.

The president's car immediately left at speed for Parkland Memorial Hospital, with Jacqueline Kennedy holding her husband's wounded head in her arms.

'Oh my God, they killed my husband!' she cried.

The cry echoed through the crowd: 'They've killed the president!'

And at one o'clock America and the rest of the world heard the news that President John Fitzgerald Kennedy was dead.

About forty-five minutes after the shooting, Dallas policeman J. D. Tippit stopped to speak to a man on the street. As Tippit got out of his car, the man pulled out a gun, shot the policeman in the head and stomach, and then ran away.

At 2.50 p.m., 24-year-old Lee Harvey Oswald was arrested in a cinema for the murder of policeman Tippit. Detectives took him to Dallas police station for questioning. Oswald said that he had not killed anyone, but a gun which had been found in the Texas Book Depository belonged to him. He was arrested again – this time for killing President Kennedy.

Jack Ruby shoots
Lee Harvey Oswald

Two days later, police decided to move Oswald from the city police building to prison. He was handcuffed to two detectives when he came out of the building, but nobody could guess what was going to happen next.

Suddenly, a man pushed his way to the front of the crowd of newspaper, radio, and television reporters. There was a gun in his hand, and seconds later he had shot Oswald in the side.

'He's been shot! Lee Harvey Oswald has been shot!' a shocked newsman told the millions of people who were watching on television.

The man with the gun was Jack Ruby, a night-club owner and a friend of local criminals – and policemen. Later he would say that he shot Oswald because he wanted to save Jacqueline Kennedy from the problems and worry of a long and painful trial.

After his own trial, he was sent to prison for life, and died in hospital in 1967.

Oswald lived for only a few hours after Jack Ruby shot him. Both Oswald and Ruby died in Parkland Memorial Hospital – the same place where Kennedy had died.

On 25 November, John Fitzgerald Kennedy was buried in Arlington National Cemetery in Washington. Jacqueline Kennedy stood with her two young children, Caroline and John, beside her, and with her husband's brothers, Robert and Edward Kennedy. America's new president, Lyndon B. Johnson, watched with the heads of other governments from all over the world. Millions more watched on television.

At the beginning, almost all Americans accepted that Lee Harvey Oswald was the single assassin, but very soon questions were asked about what had happened on that terrible day. The most important one was: how many shots were there? At first it was thought that three shots came from the sixth floor of the Texas Book Depository, where Oswald's gun was found. But some people doubted this. How could Oswald shoot three times in less than the five-and-a-half seconds? That was how long it took the president's car to pass, and it took more than two seconds to put a bullet into that kind of gun.

Then more than fifty witnesses said that they heard a fourth shot coming from a small grassy hill at the side of Elm Street, in *front* of the president's car.

There were more questions.

Did Lee Harvey Oswald assassinate the president, or was it somebody else? 'I never killed anybody!' he told the police, many times.

Was he working for someone else? The government of Cuba, perhaps, who did not like Kennedy? Or the government of the Soviet Union? Oswald had once left America to live there for a short time, before coming back with his Russian wife to Texas.

Did the group of criminals known as the Mafia kill Kennedy? They certainly wanted him dead, because he was making life difficult for them.

And so the questions, reports, books, and films go on, even today. And two interesting facts remain.

On 5 June 1968, just five years after his brother was assassinated, Robert Kennedy was shot dead at a meeting of the US Democratic Party in the Ambassador Hotel in Los Angeles. He was hoping to become President of the USA like his brother, but 24-year-old Sirhan Sirhan, a Palestinian who was living in America, got into the meeting hall and shot Robert Kennedy five times. So for a second time one of the Kennedy family was the victim of assassination.

The second fact is this. The seven men who became president in the years 1840, 1860, 1880, 1900, 1920, 1940, and 1960 all died while they were president. Four of them – Lincoln in 1860, Garfield in 1880, McKinley in 1900, and Kennedy in 1960 – were assassinated. When Ronald Reagan became president in 1980, some people wondered if he was going to die as president too. In fact, Reagan was shot by John Hinckley Junior in 1981, but he survived. Reagan broke the pattern, and was the first US president who did not die when shot by an assassin.

6   Patty Hearst

In 1974, nineteen-year-old Patty Hearst was a student at Berkeley University, in California, USA. She was also the daughter of Randolph Hearst, the rich owner of several newspapers. Patty lived in an apartment in Bienvenue Street in Berkeley with her boyfriend, Steven Weed, who was a teacher at the university.

On the evening of 4 February, two men broke into the apartment, knocked Steven on the head, and pulled Patty out of the apartment building to a car which was waiting outside.

For the next three days her parents waited by the phone, hoping to hear from the kidnappers. Then a local radio

Patty Hearst in 1973

station received the first message from a group calling themselves the Symbionese Liberation Army (SLA) – a small but dangerous group of terrorists. The leader of the SLA used the name 'Cinque', but his real name was Donald DeFreeze, and he was a criminal who had escaped from prison. Other members of the group were Nancy Ling Perry, William Wolfe, Camilla Hall, William and Emily Harris, Patricia Soltysik, and Angela Attwood.

DeFreeze said that Patty Hearst was now a prisoner of the SLA. Soon afterwards, a cassette with Patty's voice on it was sent to the radio station. She told her parents that she was all right and that the kidnappers were not hurting her.

First the gang said that they would let Patty go if two SLA members were let out of prison. That was not possible, so their next message was an order to Patty's father, Randolph Hearst. They told him that he must give seventy dollars worth of food to everyone in California who was 'on welfare' – people on welfare were those who were unable to work, or could not find work, and were getting money from the government for their basic needs. There were about six million of them in California.

Hearst refused. It would cost more than 400 million dollars, he said, and he wasn't rich enough to pay out that much money. But he did give 2 million dollars to start an organization called 'People in Need', which gave food to poor people in California. It was not enough for the kidnappers, and Patty remained a prisoner.

Or did she?

On 3 April another cassette arrived with a message from Patty. This time she told her parents that she had joined the SLA and was not a prisoner any more. She said that her name was now 'Tania', that she was fighting for the freedom of all black people, and that she would never again live with her parents, or people like them. She was now a member of the terrorist gang.

But did she join them to save her own life? That was what her parents believed. Or was she telling the truth about wanting to help the gang? It was a question that would be asked many times in the future.

The answer seemed to come on 15 April, when she and others from the gang robbed the Hibernia Bank in San Francisco. Cameras inside the bank took pictures of Patty holding a gun and telling customers to get down on the floor.

Patty in the Hibernia Bank

A few weeks later two gang members, William and Emily Harris, were caught stealing from a sports shop in Los Angeles. They only managed to get away when Patty, who had been waiting in a van across the street, used a gun to help them. Nobody was hurt, but all three of the gang escaped in the van. By now the police and many other people were sure that Patty Hearst was a criminal, not a victim.

Later, police heard from someone close to the gang that the terrorists were living at 1466 East 54th Street in Los Angeles. On 17 May more than three hundred policemen with guns were sent to the building, and the gang were told to come out with their hands up. The police fired tear gas into the house, but the terrorists replied by shooting at the police. There was a forty-minute gun battle with over 6,000 shots. TV cameras followed the battle, and millions of Americans watched.

Then the house caught fire, and Camilla Hall and Nancy Ling Perry tried to run from the house, but both were shot by the police.

Patricia Soltysik, Angela Attwood, and William Wolfe were burned to death in the fire, but Donald DeFreeze appeared to have shot himself in the head before the fire could kill him. But the bodies of Patty Hearst and William and Emily Harris were not found in the building on East 54th Street. They had not been in the house at the time.

More than a year passed before Patty Hearst was finally caught. She was arrested with Emily and William Harris in an apartment in San Francisco in September 1975. During that year the three of them had robbed two banks, and Emily Harris had killed a customer in one of them.

Patty Hearst was sent for trial in February 1976. She told the jury that everything she had done was to try and stop

The fire at East 54th Street

the SLA from killing her. She said that they had given her drugs and locked her in a cupboard for several weeks until she agreed to do what they said. By then, she said, she was so ill that she was ready to believe and say anything that they told her.

But the jury – seven of whom were women – found her guilty of bank robbery, and Patty Hearst was sent to prison in March 1976 for seven years.

Her parents worked hard to get her free, and slowly the public came to believe that Patty Hearst was not completely to blame for everything she had done. And on 1 February 1979, she walked out of prison a free woman. She wrote a book called *Every Secret Thing* about her experiences with the SLA, then went on to act in films.

7 Azaria Chamberlain

On 17 August 1980, Michael Chamberlain and his family were enjoying a holiday at Uluru. They had left their home in Mount Isa, in northern Queensland, four days earlier and had arrived at the big rock in the Australian desert late on the night of 16 August. Michael and his wife Lindy had three children: Aidan, aged six, Reagan aged four, and baby Azaria who was just ten weeks old. In the evening Michael, Lindy, and the children joined other campers for a meal outdoors. Soon after 8 p.m., Lindy put Reagan and Azaria to bed in

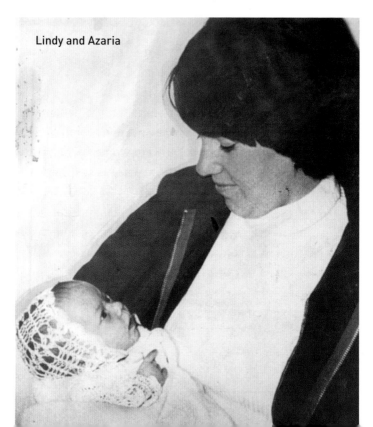

Lindy and Azaria

their tent. Some minutes after Lindy returned to the others, there was a cry from the tent. Lindy hurried across to check on the children.

Moments later, there was a scream. 'My God! My God! The dingo's got my baby!'

Lindy Chamberlain's cry was soon reported in newspapers around the world. But was it the cry of a mother who had lost her baby to one of Australia's wild dogs? Or was it a lie to cover up the murder of her ten-week-old daughter?

A dingo had been seen near the camp earlier in the evening, and the other campers immediately began a search – all except Michael Chamberlain, who told another camper, 'She's probably dead now.' The searchers found dingo footprints but no baby. One person discovered footprints of a large dingo, then found a place in the sand where something had rested for a while, but that was all.

A week later, a tourist called Wally Goodwin was near Uluru photographing wild flowers when he found some torn baby's clothes. He told the police, who took the clothes away.

Soon after, police began to have doubts about Lindy's story. The baby's clothes were found near a place where the family had walked earlier in the day. Perhaps Lindy or Michael had left them there. None of the other campers had actually seen baby Azaria the day that she disappeared, they had only seen Lindy holding something in white clothes. Perhaps it was a baby – but perhaps not.

Newspapers began to suggest reasons for baby Azaria's death. Michael Chamberlain worked for the Seventh-day Adventist Church in Mount Isa. Was the church involved in the baby's death? Some newspapers thought that perhaps the Chamberlains had killed their child because the church

Searching around the Uluru camp

had told them to do this. And when the Chamberlains appeared on television, people said that they did not look or sound like a couple who had lost their daughter in a terrible accident.

At the first inquest in Alice Springs, on 16 December 1980, police said that the damage to the baby's clothes was not the sort of damage that a dingo could do. They said too that the clothes had been removed from the child by a person, not an animal. In the end, though, the coroner decided that Azaria 'met her death when attacked by a wild dingo while asleep in her family's tent.' But because of questions about the baby's clothes, the coroner also said that someone had taken Azaria's body from the dingo and got rid of it. Who had done this, and how they had done it, was not known. This coroner did *not* find the Chamberlains responsible for the death of their child.

It did not stop the police suspecting Lindy Chamberlain of killing her child. They searched the Chamberlains' home and took away clothes. They took away the car that the

family had travelled in to Uluru. When they discovered a lot of 'blood' in the car, the police asked for a second inquest in Alice Springs. It opened a year after the first inquest, on 14 December 1981. At the end of this inquest, Coroner Gerry P. Galvin said that Lindy Chamberlain must be charged with Azaria's murder, and Michael must be charged as an accessory.

The trial of Lindy and Michael Chamberlain began on 13 September 1982. By this time, Lindy was expecting another baby. There were nine men and three women on the jury. Prosecutor Ian Barker told them that Azaria had died quickly because somebody had cut open her neck, and that Lindy Chamberlain's story about the dingo was a lie.

Witnesses said that the holes in Azaria's clothing were

A dingo

not made by teeth but by a knife, and that the blood in the Chamberlain's car was from a baby. Amy Whittaker was one of the other campers on the night that Azaria went missing. She told the jurors that the Chamberlains had walked away from the camp and were gone for nearly twenty minutes. Enough time, the prosecution said later, for the couple to find a place and bury their baby. Someone heard Lindy Chamberlain say that whatever happened, it was what God wanted.

When it was Lindy Chamberlain's turn to give evidence, she cried as she told the court what Azaria had been wearing on the night that she disappeared. But she could not explain why there was blood in the family car, or why there was not a lot of blood in the tent after an attack by a dingo.

Michael Chamberlain was questioned about how he behaved immediately after Azaria disappeared. Why did he not join the others in the search for his child? Was it because he knew that his wife had already killed his daughter? It was difficult to believe him when he simply said, 'No.'

Lawyers for Lindy Chamberlain argued that she had no reason to kill her child. She had been happy when her daughter was born, following the birth of two sons. There was also the baby's cry from the tent, heard clearly by camper Sally Lowe. How was that possible if Azaria was already dead in the Chamberlain's car? But when the jury came back into court on 29 October, they found Lindy guilty of murder. They also found Michael Chamberlain guilty of being an accessory. Lindy was sent to prison for life, but the judge said that Michael would only go to prison if he later became guilty of another crime.

A month after she went to prison, Lindy had a daughter, Kahlia. Then, in the months that followed, people began to question some of the prosecution's evidence. It now seemed that the 'blood' in the Chamberlain's car could have been a special paint used by the car maker.

Lindy's friends wrote 'Free Lindy' letters to the newspapers and to people in government. There were meetings all over the country, saying that Lindy should be let out of prison. But there were still many Australians who believed that she was guilty of killing Azaria.

Then on a January evening in 1986, a young Englishman called David Brett was killed when he fell from Uluru in a climbing accident. Some time later, when the police found his body, they also found a baby's white coat. It was Azaria's – and Brett had fallen near a place that dingoes were known to visit.

With this fresh evidence showing that her story could be true, Lindy Chamberlain was let out of prison a month

Lindy with Michael after leaving prison

later, and the court said that she was not guilty of murder. At a third inquest, in December 1995, the coroner said that nobody could say how baby Azaria died.

The story of Lindy and her daughter was made into the film *A Cry in the Dark*, starring Meryl Streep and Sam Neill. Lindy also wrote a book called *Through My Eyes: The Lindy Chamberlain Story*.

Lindy and Michael Chamberlain were divorced in 1991. In December 1992, Lindy married an American called Rick Creighton, who was also a Seventh-day Adventist. For some years they lived in Seattle, in the USA, but they now live in Australia. Michael Chamberlain has remarried, and now teaches English and History in northern New South Wales.

When Azaria died, many people thought that dingoes never attacked babies or children in this way. Since then, however, there have been other cases. In April 1998, Alan and Sharyn Rowles were on holiday at Australia's Fraser Island when a dingo tried to take their thirteen-month-old daughter away. Luckily, the dingo dropped the baby when Mr Rowles chased it. In 2001, two children aged nine and seven were attacked by dingoes near a camp at Waddy Point. The older boy died. So attacks by dingoes are rare, but they do happen.

The whole story of Azaria Chamberlain remains a mystery, as her body has never been found.

* In June 2012, at a fourth inquest, coroner Elizabeth Morris decided that a dingo had taken Azaria Chamberlain from the tent, and that Lindy Chamberlain was not guilty of killing her daughter. The case is now closed.

8   Shergar

Shergar's name had often been in the newspapers. In 1981 the powerful brown horse won one of the most famous horse races in the world, the Epsom Derby, which has been held in England since 1780. An excited crowd saw Shergar pass the finishing post 24 metres ahead of the other horses. No horse had ever won the race by so big a distance. That year he was European Horse of the Year, but after six wins he stopped racing because of injury.

In 1983 Shergar was living at the Ballymany horse farm near Newbridge in Ireland. Although his racing days were over, Shergar was still very valuable, because he could father

Shergar wins the Epsom Derby

many successful racehorses in future years. Nobody knew that Shergar's name would soon be in the newspapers for quite a different reason. He would be the first victim of a horse kidnapping in Ireland.

For James Fitzgerald, the man who looked after Shergar at Ballymany, it all began at about 8.45 p.m. on Tuesday 8 February 1983. Two men with guns, their faces covered by balaclavas, pushed their way into his house and locked Mr Fitzgerald's wife, son, and daughter in a downstairs room. Then they ordered him to take them to Shergar's special stable, and to open the stable door. At the same time other members of the gang were driving a car and horsebox to the stable.

After opening the stable door, Fitzgerald was ordered to lead the horse into the horsebox, and Shergar went in quietly. Then Fitzgerald was pushed into a van with some more of the kidnappers and told to lie down with his face on the floor.

The gang drove around for several hours, and finally let Fitzgerald go about 40 kilometres away from the farm. 'We want 2 million pounds for the horse,' they said. They told him not to contact the police, and said that they would telephone him the next day.

Fitzgerald telephoned his boss – the manager of the Ballymany farm – as soon as he got home, and the police were informed about the kidnapping in the early hours of the next morning. Fitzgerald was questioned, but he could tell detectives very little about the kidnappers. They had all worn balaclavas and he did not know what any of them looked like. Cleverly, the gang had chosen a day for the kidnapping when there were hundreds of horseboxes on the roads, travelling to one of Ireland's biggest horse sales.

Shergar after his racing days

Nobody would notice or remember one more horsebox with a brown horse inside.

Soon newspaper, television, and radio reporters had the news, and everyone learned that one of the world's most famous racehorses had been kidnapped.

The police searched stables and farm buildings across the whole of Ireland, and *The Sporting Life* racing newspaper offered 10,000 pounds for Shergar's safe return. There were phone calls between the gang and the office of Shergar's owners, but after four days the calls stopped.

Weeks and months went by. During this time, hundreds of people telephoned the police to say that they thought they had seen the famous racehorse – either in fields, on roads, or in vans – in various parts of the world. Others phoned to say that they were holding Shergar and would cut off his head unless money was paid to them. There were two telephone calls to an Irish radio station, saying that Shergar would be returned because 1.2 million pounds had been paid to the kidnappers in France, but these were quickly proved to be false.

By October that year, Shergar's owners were offering 100,000 pounds for his safe return, but there was no news.

There is still no news, but there are a number of different ideas about what happened to Shergar. Some people say the IRA (the Irish Republican Army) was responsible for the kidnapping, and this explanation is probably the best one. The IRA needed money, and the horse's owners were very rich. But the gang were not experienced at working with horses. Perhaps the frightened horse injured himself and had to be shot. Once he was dead, Shergar was worth nothing, so the gang stopped trying to collect the money. And Shergar's owners were not planning to pay any money to the kidnappers. They knew that if they did, horses everywhere could be the next victims.

To remember this great horse, special races are held every year at Ascot in England on a day in August. Teams from Great Britain, Ireland, Europe, and the Rest of the World ride in six races to try to get the most points and win the Shergar Cup. But Shergar's body has never been found, and millions of people will remember him as the horse that disappeared.

9 Bonnie and Clyde

In January 1930, two young people visited a friend in West Dallas, Texas. One of them was nineteen-year-old Bonnie Parker, the other was twenty-year-old Clyde Barrow. They had never met before and knew nothing about each other, but together they soon became two of the most famous criminals in the history of America. They robbed stores and banks in Texas, Oklahoma, Missouri, Louisiana, and New Mexico. Their pictures were in the newspapers and their names were on the radio. Long after they were dead, there would be books, magazine stories, films, and songs about them.

So who were they?

Bonnie Elizabeth Parker was born in Rowena, Texas, on 1 October 1910. She was the second of three children. Her father died when she was four years old, and her mother moved the family to West Dallas where they lived with Bonnie's grandmother. Bonnie grew up to be a pretty young woman, just 150 cm tall with fair hair. She was also a clever student, and an excellent writer.

A week before her sixteenth birthday, she married Roy

Bonnie and Clyde

Thornton. It was not a successful marriage. Roy was a thief, and he would disappear for several weeks at a time. The couple separated in January 1929, and not long after that, Roy was arrested during a robbery at Red Oak, Texas. He was sent to Huntsville prison for five years. At the time Bonnie was working as a waitress in Marco's café in West Dallas, but in October 1929 the café closed and Bonnie was without a job.

Clyde Barrow was born on 21 March 1909 in Telico, Texas. He was one of eight children. The family had a farm until Clyde was twelve years old and then they moved to West Dallas. Clyde's father began buying and selling anything he could find to earn money. After a time, he went to work at a garage.

In 1926, when Clyde was seventeen, he hired a car. He was late returning it to the car hire company, so they informed the police, and Clyde was arrested. But he persuaded the police that it was all a mistake and they let him go. Soon after that Clyde and his brother Buck began stealing things from stores, and then came car thefts and burglary. The police often suspected Buck and Clyde of these crimes, but could not prove anything.

Bonnie fell in love with Clyde almost as soon as they met. They began to see each other, and Clyde visited Bonnie's home. It was there that the police arrested him in February 1930 for stealing cars and for several burglaries. This time they had proof, and he was sent to prison for two years in Kaufman, Texas. To his surprise, he met an old friend called William Turner there.

When Bonnie visited Clyde in prison, he introduced her to Turner, and asked her to help them escape. Turner told her about a gun which he kept at his parents' house. Bonnie agreed to get the gun for him, and secretly got the gun into the prison. Clyde and Turner, and another prisoner called Emory Abernathy, used it to make their escape.

Clyde could not return to Bonnie immediately because the police were watching her. He stole a car with Turner and Abernathy and they began to travel across Texas, Missouri, and Illinois. The police caught them in Middletown, Ohio, and Clyde was sent to Eastham Prison Farm, Huntsville, for fourteen years. He was allowed to leave in February 1932 after his mother took his case back to court, and was soon back with Bonnie.

But this was a difficult time in America. Thousands of honest, hard-working men and women could not find work. After a short time helping his father at the garage, Clyde went back to his life of crime and stole a car with Bonnie. The police chased them and caught Bonnie, but Clyde escaped. Bonnie was sent to prison in Kaufman for two months.

Then, on 13 April, Clyde and two friends – Ted Rogers and a man called Johnny – robbed a store. The owner, John Bucher, was shot and killed. Although Clyde said that he was waiting for the others in the car at the time of the shooting, he became 'wanted for murder'. The three criminals went their separate ways.

In June 1932, Bonnie finished her time in prison. In August she was visiting her mother when Clyde and Raymond Hamilton killed a policeman in Stringtown, Oklahoma. Hamilton was an old friend of Clyde's and had recently come out of prison. The two men were sitting in a stolen car outside a dance hall drinking whisky when Sheriffs C. G. Maxwell and Eugene C. Moore saw them. At this time strong drinks like whisky were not allowed in the USA, and the two policemen went to investigate. Clyde shot at them, killing Moore and injuring Maxwell, and the two young criminals escaped.

Clyde and Hamilton drove all night, finally leaving the car in the small town of Grandview, south of Dallas. Not long after this, Hamilton was caught in Michigan and was sent back to prison in Dallas.

During the late summer of 1932, Bonnie and Clyde were suspected of nearly every bank and store robbery in Texas. Then, in December of that year, they were joined by sixteen-year-old William Daniel Jones. 'W. D.' became the third member of the 'Barrow Gang', as the papers had started to call them.

On the evening of 26 January 1933, Police Officer Tom Persell saw three people in a Ford V-8 car. He thought that they looked like car thieves, so he followed them on his motorcycle. It was a mistake. When the Ford V-8 stopped, Persell stopped behind it. Suddenly, W. D. Jones got out of the car with a gun in his hand.

'Get into the car, or I'll kill you,' W. D. said.

Many hours later, the three young criminals let the police officer go. But Persell knew that he was lucky to be alive.

Then, in March 1933, Clyde's brother Buck came out of prison. Buck and his wife Blanche arranged to meet with Clyde, Bonnie, and W. D. Jones in Joplin, Missouri, where they took an apartment. But neighbours began to ask questions. Why did the gang have so many guns? Why did they stay in the apartment with the curtains closed? News soon reached the police about the mysterious new people in town.

The police arrived at the apartment, and almost at once a deadly gun battle began. Two policemen were killed, and Clyde and W. D. were both shot and injured. But all five of the gang escaped.

After they had gone, the police found photographs of the gang in the apartment. One photograph, which showed Bonnie with a cigar, became very famous. By now stories about Bonnie and Clyde were appearing in newspapers all across the country. Millions of Americans followed their adventures with excitement. At a time when jobs were few and life was miserable, here were people living a wild life with plenty of money, fast cars, and guns. Bonnie and Clyde were young, in love – and they even 'kidnapped' the police! They were clever, too: after a robbery, they would quickly cross into the next state. Police from one state were not allowed to leave their own state and cross into a different one when chasing criminals, so Bonnie and Clyde often escaped this way.

One day, Clyde sent W. D. Jones to steal a Chevrolet car from outside a house in Ruston, Louisiana. The owner, a Mr Darby, saw W. D. driving away in his car, and quickly asked his friend Sofia Stone for help. They jumped into Miss Stone's car and immediately began to chase after the Chevrolet.

It was soon clear to them that Miss Stone's car could not go fast enough, so they turned back. Minutes later, they were surprised to see a Ford V-8 chasing *them*. Clyde was driving, and Bonnie, Buck, and Blanche were with him. The criminals made Darby and Miss Stone get out of her car and into theirs. They drove all night, stopping only for food. Next day, on a country road outside of Waldo, Arkansas, Clyde let Darby and Miss Stone go.

'Call the sheriff,' Clyde told them, laughing. 'He'll give you a ride home.'

The gang's next big problem came when Clyde was driving a stolen Ford V-8 car near Wellington in Texas. He was driving too fast, and the car crashed. Bonnie was trapped under the car when it caught fire. A farmer, Tom Pritchard, and his wife rescued her, but someone phoned the police. The gang saw them coming and got away in Pritchard's car.

Clyde's brother Buck

Things really began to go wrong when they took some rooms at the Red Crown Tourist Camp in Platte City, Missouri. Clyde went to a store in town to buy medicine for Bonnie's injured leg. But news about the accident and Bonnie's injury had reached Platte City, and the store owner told police about Clyde's visit and the medicine he had bought.

The police went to the tourist camp and the usual gun battle followed. This time, Buck was hit in the head, but not killed. Blanche was hit in the eye by flying glass after a bullet hit the car window as the gang escaped. But they were discovered three days later, in a park in Dexter, Iowa. There was a car chase, and this time Clyde crashed the gang's car into a tree. Police shot at the car and Buck was hit several more times. He and Blanche were captured by the police, but Clyde, Bonnie and W. D. Jones got away.

After a few days, Buck died from his injuries in hospital. Blanche was sent to prison in Missouri for ten years.

Some months later, W. D. decided to leave what was left of the gang, but when he got to Texas he was caught by the police. He told them that Bonnie and Clyde had held him prisoner to stop him from informing on them.

In the following January, Clyde and some friends helped Raymond Hamilton and Henry Methvin to escape from the Eastham Prison Farm in Texas. Two guards were shot during the escape. The 'new' gang spent the next few months robbing more banks and stores. Then, in March, Hamilton left them.

On Easter Sunday, in April 1934, Clyde and Methvin shot and killed two police officers in Grapevine, Texas. On 6 April Bonnie and Clyde killed another policeman in Commerce, Oklahoma. They also captured the Chief of Police, Percy Boyd, but later let him go.

After the Grapevine murders, people's opinion of Bonnie and Clyde began to change. Too many policemen were dying, and something had to be done. The chief of Texas prisons, Lee Simmons, was angry about the deaths of the two guards at Eastham Prison Farm. He hired an officer called Captain Frank Hamer to find Bonnie and Clyde. But Hamer always arrived at places just after the young criminals had left.

Then Lee Simmons got a visit from Ivy Methvin, Henry's father. He wanted a free pardon for his son in return for helping to capture Bonnie and Clyde. At this time Bonnie and Clyde and Henry were living in an empty house in the woods near Bienville Parish, near the home of Henry's parents.

On 21 May 1934, Bonnie and Clyde stayed at the house while Henry Methvin went to see his parents. Henry's father told him about the free pardon. Henry agreed to help, and the police began to make plans.

At 9.10 a.m. on 23 May 1934, Bonnie and Clyde were driving back to the house in the woods from the small town of Gibsland. Henry was not with them. He had stayed in town, because he knew what was going to happen. Clyde was driving his favourite kind of car – a stolen Ford V-8. As they came to the top of a hill Clyde saw a truck that he recognized at the side of the road. It was Ivy Methvin's truck, and Ivy was standing beside it.

Hamer and his men were hidden in the trees nearby. They watched as Clyde stopped the Ford V-8 next to Ivy's truck. They saw Ivy Methvin suddenly run into the woods. It was the signal for Hamer and his men to start shooting.

Clyde was killed with the first bullet. Bonnie started to scream, but seconds later she was dead too. But still the bullets kept coming through the car windows and doors. The police wanted to be sure.

Death for Bonnie and Clyde

And so the deadly adventures of Bonnie and Clyde were over. Clyde Barrow was buried in Western Heights, West Dallas, next to his brother Buck, on May 25, 1934. Bonnie's mother refused to let Bonnie be buried next to Clyde. She was buried at Crown Hill in West Dallas two days later.

Henry Methvin got his free pardon in Texas, but then went to prison in Oklahoma for twelve years for his part in the murder in Commerce. He was killed by a train in 1948. Blanche Barrow was then the only one of the gang still alive. After leaving prison she married again, and lived a quiet life until her death in 1988.

Bonnie and Clyde had four wild years together, with gun fights, robberies, and car chases. But nine policemen had died, and the young couple knew that their story could only end one way. During her short life, Bonnie often wrote poems. Some time in the last few weeks of her life, she wrote a poem called 'The Story of Bonnie and Clyde'. It ended like this:

Someday they'll go down together
And they'll bury them side by side
To few it'll be grief, to the law a relief
But it's death for Bonnie and Clyde.

10   Nick Leeson

It began with a mistake of 20,000 pounds in July 1992, and ended in February 1995 with losses of 800 million pounds. A clever but dishonest young man had managed to hide what he was doing from his employers until it was too late – *much* too late. In the disaster that followed, one of Britain's oldest banks had to close, and 1,200 people lost their jobs.

Nick Leeson grew up in Watford, north of London. His first job, in 1985, was with the bank Coutts and Company. He stayed with them for two years, then moved to the American bank Morgan Stanley. In July 1989, he joined Barings Bank, which had begun in London in 1762 and had had many of the kings and queens of Britain as its customers. After working in the London offices for a time he was sent to Jakarta, in Indonesia, then was made General Manager at the bank's Singapore offices in March 1992. He hired traders and office workers, and became Chief Trader himself. While in Jakarta, he had met Lisa Sims and they were married shortly before the move to Singapore.

Leeson was successful and popular, and made millions of pounds for the bank. As a result, managers at Barings' London offices left him to do his job with almost no checks on his work. This made it simple for him to hide the very big losses that he would make over the next three years.

On Friday, 17 July 1992, Leeson discovered a mistake made by Kim Wong, one of his staff. She had sold twenty contracts instead of buying them, a mistake that would cost Barings 20,000 pounds. Leeson made an error account – a

Nick Leeson at school, 1983

secret place where he could keep bank information – and hid the mistake in it. This was the famous Error Account 88888 (some people believe that 88888 is a very lucky number).

By 1993, Leeson had made more than 10 million pounds for Barings, about 10 per cent of the bank's profits for that year. In the bank's eyes he was a star, and he earned an extra 130,000 pounds as well as his pay of 50,000 pounds. He and Lisa had a beautiful flat and went on holiday to fashionable places.

But then things began to go wrong, as Leeson's luck began to change. By the end of 1994, his losses were more than 200 million pounds, all hidden in Error Account 88888. Leeson went on spending millions of pounds on contracts, hoping that he could sell them later at a profit and clear his losses. It didn't work. His losses continued to grow.

On 23 February 1995, two days before his twenty-eighth birthday, trader Nick Leeson cleared his desk in the Singapore offices of Barings and went on the run. He left behind him a note saying 'I'm sorry', and losses of 800 million pounds – enough to put the bank out of business.

He then took Lisa to Kuala Lumpur where they stayed overnight at the Regent Hotel. Lisa knew nothing about his problems at this time. Next day they flew to Kota Kinabalu on the north coast of Borneo. Two days later, in the little shop of the hotel where they were staying, a man walked past Nick carrying a copy of the *New Straits Times* newspaper. Nick saw the headline: BRITISH MERCHANT BANK COLLAPSES.

'Lisa, buy that paper,' he said. 'Pay cash. Don't sign anything.'

They went back to their bedroom and read the report in the paper. Police were looking for a missing trader.

'Is the missing trader you?' Lisa asked her husband.

'Yes,' Nick said. 'I've been trying to tell you. I lost them a lot of money.'

Leeson knew that he would go to prison, but he did not want that prison to be in South East Asia. He wanted to get back to England. He and Lisa tried to get a plane to London but could only get a flight to Frankfurt in Germany.

'How much is a one-way ticket?' Leeson asked. He wasn't planning to come back.

Everyone on the plane seemed to be reading newspapers, and every newspaper seemed to have Leeson's picture on the front. He was one of the world's most wanted men. They

Leeson under arrest in Germany

landed at Frankfurt airport in the early hours of the morning – and saw the German police waiting for them.

Leeson spent nearly nine months in prison in Frankfurt, and then in November 1995 he was sent back to Singapore for trial. He was sent to prison for six and a half years. Meanwhile, Barings Bank had had to close, and 1,200 people lost their jobs. Barings was sold to a Dutch bank for one pound.

Leeson in 2004

While in prison, Leeson became seriously ill with cancer, but with the help of doctors he survived. By the time he left prison in 1999, Lisa had divorced him and married someone else.

Leeson returned to Britain in 1999 without a job or a home, but he has made a new life for himself. He now lives in Galway, in Ireland. He has married again, and he and his wife, Leona, have three children (two from her first marriage). In 2005, Leeson became General Manager of Galway United Football Club. He speaks at dinners and meetings all over the world, and has written two books: *Rogue Trader* (which was made into a film starring Ewan McGregor) and *Back from the Brink*. He is without doubt a survivor.

11 Charles Ponzi and Elmyr de Hory

One great idea – and a little luck. Sometimes that is all it takes to make a millionaire. Charles Ponzi and Elmyr de Hory both had ideas that would bring them a lot of money. But things did not go exactly as they had hoped.

Charles Ponzi In December 1919, Charles Ponzi was a young man with very little money who had just started a business in Boston, USA. Just six months later, Ponzi and his wife Rose were living in a twenty-room house with a swimming pool, and crowds of people waited outside his office every day, hoping to put money into his business. In the month of May alone he took 420,000 dollars. What was Ponzi's secret?

Ponzi had always dreamed of making a lot of money. He was born in Italy in 1882, and went to university in Rome, but did not finish his studies. In 1903 he sailed to the United States and arrived in Boston with just two dollars and fifty cents in his pocket. Over the next fifteen years he worked in restaurants, offices and banks, but he also spent time in a prison in Canada for stealing a cheque. He tried different ideas to make money, but without success. Then he discovered the international reply coupon, and his dream of becoming rich and famous started to come true.

An international reply coupon, or IRC, was a small piece of printed paper that you could buy in one country and send inside a letter to someone in another country. The second

person could use the coupon to buy stamps for their reply. Ponzi learned that IRCs were cheaper in Italy than in the USA. His plan was this: send money to friends in Italy; get them to buy IRCs and send them to the USA; change the IRCs to stamps; sell the stamps. In this way, Ponzi thought he could make a profit of 400 per cent or more.

He started a business called the Securities Exchange Company, and began to tell friends about the scheme. 'Give me 100 dollars,' he said, 'and in forty-five days I'll give you 150 dollars.' The news travelled quickly through Boston, and soon there were queues of people outside his office, crazy with hope and excitement. On busy days, twenty police officers, six of them on horseback, were needed to control the crowds. Some people invested all their money in his business. After forty-five days he paid his investors the money he had promised, but many of them put it back into the business straight away. By July Ponzi's office was collecting 200,000 dollars a day.

Then people began to ask questions. Where was the profit coming from? How many IRCs did Ponzi have? Information about Ponzi's criminal past added to their worries. Angry crowds came to the office of the Securities Exchange Company. Everyone wanted their money back, and fighting began in the queues. Ponzi came out and spoke to people, gave them coffee, and returned money to people who asked for it. Many of them changed their minds and left their money in the business.

But by the middle of August it was all over. On Friday 13 August 1920, police arrested Ponzi and took him to prison. Surprisingly, a lot of his investors continued to believe in him after his arrest. In November he was sentenced to five years in prison for fraud. Nobody had bought any IRCs in Italy, and Ponzi had not invested any money or made any profit. He had simply taken the money that came in from new investors, and paid it to investors who had waited for forty-five days and wanted their profit. Sooner or later, it had to end.

The mystery is that Ponzi did not take his millions and escape to another country before he was arrested. It seems that he hoped to use the money to make a real business that would make him and his investors rich. It is thought that Ponzi collected about 10 million dollars from his thousands of investors. After years of hard work, investigators were able to return some of the money, but it was less than half of what was invested.

It was not the end of Ponzi's schemes. When he came out of prison he went to Florida, where he and his wife bought land with two friends. They would buy a piece of land for 16 dollars, divide it into twenty-three parts, and sell each part for 10 dollars – a profit of 214 dollars. But the police soon became interested in this scheme – because some of the land was under water! Ponzi ran away from Florida, but was found and returned to Boston, where he had to go to prison once again.

He finally left prison in 1934, and was sent back to Italy. Rose divorced him and stayed in the USA. After a time Ponzi went to Brazil, where he worked for an Italian airline, but in his last years he was a poor man, earning a little money now and then from giving English lessons. He died in 1949.

Few people remember Charles Ponzi now, but he has given his name to the 'Ponzi scheme'. There are still plenty of these in the world today, promising to 'Make money fast!' and give you 'Fantastic profits!' But on a US government website you can find this warning about Ponzi schemes. If you begin with 1,000 investors, and you promise them 100 per cent profit, you need 2,000 new investors to pay them their profit. Next time you need 4,000 new investors – and each time you need a bigger number of new investors. When you have done this sixteen times, you need more new investors than there are people in the world! So if it sounds too good to be true, it is probably a Ponzi scheme.

Charles Ponzi leaving prison

Elmyr de Hory   There are many ways to make money from art, but few painters become millionaires. People will pay millions of pounds for paintings by great artists, but it is much harder for a new artist, even a good one, to make a living. It is not surprising, then, that sometimes clever artists decide that there is a better future in fakes than in their own work.

In 1987 one of Vincent Van Gogh's *Sunflowers* paintings was bought by Japanese businessman Yasuo Goto for 25 million pounds. But to this day, art specialists cannot agree whether it is a real Van Gogh, a copy by his friend Gauguin, or a fake. Certainly there are thousands of fakes in museums, galleries, and the homes of rich people all over the world. The French painter Corot was very popular in the early twentieth century, and in 1940 *Newsweek* magazine said, 'Of the 2,500 paintings Corot did in his lifetime, 7,800 are to be found in America.' Elmyr de Hory was extraordinarily good at making fakes, and his work made a lot of money – but much of it went into the pockets of other people.

De Hory was born in Hungary in 1906, and studied art in Budapest and then Munich in Germany. In 1926 he moved to Paris, where he studied under the painter Fernand Léger. Though de Hory did well in his studies, he also enjoyed meeting artists and writers and living a wild life. After some years he decided to return to Hungary, but he had a difficult time before and during the Second World War, spending much of it in prison.

In 1946 he returned to Paris where he began to paint again. Soon he discovered that his copies of Picasso paintings were so good that his friends thought they were real. After selling one to a friend, he began to take his 'Picassos' to galleries. Here he was lucky. After the war many people found that they needed money, so they would take valuable things like paintings or silver and sell them. Nobody asked questions when de Hory arrived with Picassos which he said had belonged to his family in Hungary. He was also clever in the way he worked: he did not make copies of real Picassos, but painted new paintings that looked exactly like Picasso's work.

Later that year de Hory began to work with a friend, Jacques Chamberlin. At first this worked well; Chamberlin organized the business while de Hory did the paintings. Together they travelled through Europe and South America, selling the paintings and living the good life. They stayed in the best hotels and ate in expensive restaurants. But de Hory discovered that Chamberlin was lying about the prices he got for the paintings, and was keeping most of the money for himself. This was a problem that de Hory would have many times; it was easy for others to cheat him when they had contact with the buyers and de Hory did not. De Hory went back to working alone.

In 1947 he visited the United States and liked it so much that he decided to stay there. He bought an apartment in Miami and travelled to New York, Los Angeles, and other cities selling his paintings. Sometimes de Hory would stop making forgeries and instead try to sell his own paintings, but he was never successful at this. But there were dangers in forgery, and some galleries were beginning to suspect that de Hory's paintings were fakes. He began to study other painters, like Matisse, Modigliani, and Renoir, so he could offer paintings by different artists. He also began to sell his work by post, and to use false names.

When one of his customers wanted to take him to court over a fake painting in 1955, de Hory escaped to Mexico, where he got into more trouble. The police said he had been involved in a murder, and tried to get money from him. De Hory hired a lawyer, who also tried to get money from him. But de Hory had the last laugh. He paid the lawyer with one of his paintings – a fake, of course – and left before the lawyer realized what had happened.

But on his return to the USA, he found that his fakes were selling for extraordinarily high prices, while he had little money. He became so unhappy that in 1956 he tried to kill himself, but he was found and taken to hospital. Then he met Fernand Legros, who suggested that they should work together. Legros was an excellent salesman, but like Chamberlin, he lied to de Hory and kept too much of the profit. When de Hory moved to the Spanish island of Ibiza in 1962, Legros stayed in Paris, enjoying the profits. But de Hory was getting tired, and his fakes were not as good as they used to be. The police began to investigate his work and to watch Legros. By 1967 Legros was in prison for fraud, and in 1968 de Hory was sent to prison in Spain for two months.

When he came out, he was famous. Clifford Irving wrote a book called *Fake!* which told his life story, and Orson Welles made a film about him called *F for Fake*, which was first shown in 1974. Once more de Hory tried to sell his own paintings; he made much less money from them, but they were his own work, and he was pleased that people recognized their quality.

Then he learned that the French police wanted to arrest

him for fraud. He knew that he would probably spend the rest of his life in prison, and the idea filled him with horror. On 11 December 1976 he took his own life in his home in Ibiza. So died one of the art world's greatest forgers – a clever painter who could only succeed by painting other people's paintings.

What would de Hory think now if he knew what had happened to his paintings? People now recognize that his forgeries are themselves great paintings. Then there are the paintings that de Hory did himself, which are valuable and popular works of art. But of course since his death there have been no more paintings by de Hory. Or have there? Art specialists report that it is now possible to buy fake de Horys, made by other people but sold as de Hory's work. Perhaps even de Hory would smile at that.

Elmyr de Hory

GLOSSARY

art   beautiful things like painting and drawings that someone has made; (*n*) **artist**

assassinate   to kill an important or famous person; (*n*) **assassin**

balaclava   a kind of hat that covers the head and face

camp   a place where people stay in tents in holiday

capture   to catch somebody and keep them prisoner

case   a crime that the police must investigate

cemetery   a place where dead people are buried

contract   (here) an agreement to buy or sell something in the future

coroner   the person whose job is to find the reason for a sudden or suspicious death

court   the place where trials happen; the people who hear the evidence and make decisions about crimes

courtyard   an open space surrounded by buildings

divorce   to end your marriage to somebody

doorknob   a round handle that opens a door

drug   a kind of medicine given by a doctor; something that you take to make you feel excited, happy, strong etc.

evidence   information that is used in court to try to prove something

fake (*n & adj*)   a copy of something that seems real but is not

fingerprint   the mark that a finger makes when it touches something

forge   to make an illegal copy of something

frame   a thin piece of wood or metal around the edge of a picture

fraud   the crime of cheating somebody in order to get money from them

freedom   not being in prison; being able to do what you want

gallery   a room or building where you can see paintings etc.

gang   a group of criminals who work together

glove   something you wear to keep your hand warm or safe

government a group of people who control a country

guilty having done something that is against the law

handcuffs a pair of metal rings that hold a prisoner's wrists together

hang to kill somebody by putting a rope round their neck and letting their body drop down

inquest an investigation to find out why somebody died

invest to give money to a business or bank in the hope of getting more money back; (*n*) **investor**

investigate to try to find out about something; (*n*) **investigation**

jury a group of people who listen to evidence and decide if somebody is guilty of a crime

kidnap to take somebody away and keep them as a prisoner, especially in order to get money for returning them

lorry a large vehicle for carrying heavy things by road

losses money that a business or bank loses

member somebody who belongs to a group or organization

museum a place where you can look at old or interesting things

pardon an official decision that somebody is not guilty of a crime

poison something that will make you very ill or kill you if you take it into your body; (*v*) to give somebody poison

powerful very strong; having a lot of control over people

profit the money that you make in business or by selling things

prosecution the organization that tries to show that somebody is guilty of a crime; (*n*) **prosecutor** a lawyer who works for the prosecution

race a competition to see who can run, drive etc. the fastest

scheme a plan for organizing something

sheriff (*American*) an officer who is responsible for law and order

shock a very bad surprise

signal a light used on the railways to tell drivers to stop or go slower

stable a building in which horses are kept

state a part of a country with its own government

store a shop

tear gas a gas that makes your eyes fill with tears, used by police to control crowds

tent a kind of small house made of cloth, used when camping

terrorist a person who hurts or kills people, for example with bombs, to try and make the government do what they want

trader a person who buys and sells things as a job

truck a vehicle that is open at the back, used for carrying things

van a kind of big car or small lorry for carrying things

victim someone who suffers as the result of a crime

witness a person who gives evidence in a court of law

ACTIVITIES

Before Reading

1 **Read the back cover of the book, and the introduction on the first page. Which of these words do you think you will find in the book, and why?**

shoe, farm, heart, note, drug, grandfather, glove, bread, poison, cow, insect, knife

2 **Match the crimes with the definitions.**

assassination	Using violence to steal money or other things
kidnapping	Hurting, killing, or frightening people to try to make the government do what you want
murder	Deliberately taking someone's life
robbery	Killing a political leader
terrorism	Taking someone and keeping them as a prisoner in order to get money

3 **Here are some crimes. Which do you think is the most serious, and why? How do you think the people should be punished?**

1 A man kills his wife and runs away with another woman.
2 Someone kidnaps a child and asks the parents for money.
3 A woman is forced to join a terrorist organisation, and she takes part in a bank robbery.
4 People pay thousands of dollars for paintings by Picasso – but the man who sold them painted them himself.

ACTIVITIES

While Reading

Read Chapter 1, then match these halves of sentences.

1 When Cora sang in theatres, . . .
2 Crippen could not work as a doctor in England . . .
3 Crippen fell in love with Ethel Le Neve, . . .
4 After killing Cora, Crippen told everyone that . . .
5 The police found part of a woman's body . . .
6 Ethel and Crippen travelled on the *Montrose* . . .
7 Crippen was arrested by Inspector Dew . . .
8 On the day that Crippen died, . . .

a she had gone back to America.
b Ethel sailed from London for New York.
c because he had trained in another country.
d using the name 'Robinson'.
e she called herself 'Belle Elmore'.
f under Crippen's house in London.
g who was his secretary.
h before he reached Canada.

Read Chapter 2, then answer these questions.

1 In which city is the Louvre Museum?
2 Why were people not surprised that the painting had gone?
3 What did police find on the empty picture frame?
4 How much money did the thief want for the picture?
5 What was Alfredo Geri's job?
6 What was Vincenzo Perugia's job?
7 What did police find in the thief's diary?

Read Chapter 3, then complete the sentences with the correct names.

Cemetery John / Dr Condon / Betty Gow /
Bruno Hauptmann / Charles Lindbergh /
Charles Lindbergh Junior / Violet Sharpe

1 ____ was a rich, famous pilot.
2 ____ was often called 'Little It'.
3 ____ was Charles Junior's nurse.
4 ____, who worked for the Lindberghs, killed herself a few months after the kidnapping.
5 The kidnapper arranged to meet ____ in a cemetery.
6 ____ collected 50,000 dollars for false information about the missing child.
7 ____ was found guilty of killing Charles Junior.

Read Chapter 4. Put these events in the correct order.

1 The police found some fingerprints at the farmhouse.
2 The night mail train left Glasgow for London.
3 Some robbers took bags of money out of the train.
4 Most of the robbers were caught and put in prison.
5 The robbers went to the farmhouse to count the money.
6 The train driver saw a red signal and stopped the train.
7 The robbers bought an old farmhouse.
8 Two robbers attacked the driver.

Read Chapter 5. Are these sentences true (T) or false (F)?

1 President Kennedy was shot in Texas.
2 The president was hit by a single bullet.
3 Jack Ruby killed policeman Tippit.
4 Oswald, Ruby and the president died in the same place.
5 After Kennedy's death, his brother became president.
6 Ronald Reagan did not die while he was president.

Read Chapter 6, then fill in the gaps with these words.

caught, free, guilty, member, owner, rob, terrorists, trial

Patty Hearst was the daughter of a newspaper _____. She
was kidnapped by _____. Two months later, she became
a _____ of the gang and helped them to _____ a bank.
A year later she was _____ and sent for _____. The jury
found her _____ and she was sent to prison, but a few years
later she was _____.

**Read Chapter 7, then rewrite these untrue sentences with the
correct information.**

1 The Chamberlain children were sleeping in a hotel room.
2 Lindy Chamberlain said that a lion had taken her baby.
3 At the end of the second inquest, Michael Chamberlain
   was charged with murder.
4 Lindy Chamberlain had a son while she was in prison.
5 When the police found a dead climber, they also found
   Azaria's body.
6 Lindy wrote a song, *Through My Eyes*, about her
   experience.

Read Chapter 8, then answer these questions.

1 After his injury, why was Shergar still very valuable?
2 Why couldn't Mr Fitzgerald see the kidnappers' faces?
3 What did the kidnappers do with Mr Fitzgerald's wife and
   children?
4 How much money did the kidnappers want for the horse?
5 Why were there hundreds of horseboxes on the roads when
   Shergar was kidnapped?
6 Who probably kidnapped Shergar, and why?

Read Chapter 9, then circle a, b, or c.

1 Bonnie helped Clyde and Turner to escape from ____.
   a) the police   b) prison   c) a robbery
2 The Barrow Gang ____ officer Persell.
   a) killed   b) shot   c) kidnapped
3 In the apartment in Joplin the police found ____.
   a) whisky   b) photos   c) money
4 Bonnie was hurt in a ____.
   a) car crash   b) gunfight   c) robbery
5 For helping the police, Henry Methvin got ____.
   a) a job   b) money   c) a pardon

Read Chapter 10. Choose the best question-word for these questions, and then answer them.

How many / *What* / *Where* / *Why*

1 . . . didn't managers at Barings often check Leeson's work?
2 . . . mistake did Kim Wong make?
3 . . . did Leeson hide his losses?
4 . . . did Leeson leave behind when he left Barings?
5 . . . did Leeson try to return to England?
6 . . . people lost their jobs when Barings closed?

Read Chapter 11, then fill in the gaps with these words.

America, discovered, fakes, fraud, hoped, invest, paintings, profit, schemes, worth

Ponzi and de Hory both _____ to make money in _____.
Ponzi promised to _____ people's money, and give them
the _____, but he went to prison for _____. De Hory
_____ that people would pay thousands for his _____,
but not for his own _____ . People still talk about Ponzi
_____ today, and de Hory's own paintings are now
_____ a lot of money.

ACTIVITIES

After Reading

1 **Perhaps this is what some of the people in the book are thinking. Who are they? What has happened, and what's going to happen?**

1 'I'm sure it's them. She looks just like the girl in that photo. And now they're taking us – well, who knows where! Oh, why on earth did I listen to Darby? What's going to happen to us?'

2 'This is terrifying! Those men in balaclavas – they've locked us in this room. They have guns, too! Who are they? Is this a robbery? And where have they taken my husband?'

3 'Now, how can I get out? I'll try to break open this door. Wait – someone's coming! It's one of the museum workers! Perhaps if I just sit here on the stairs . . .'

4 'Twenty thousand pounds? That's not much money. I'll hide the loss in a special account. I'll soon make enough money to cover up the mistake.'

5 'This is a mad idea! This haircut, and these boy's clothes! The captain keeps looking at me. I'm sure he suspects something. I'll be glad when we get to Canada!'

6 'That's strange. Why is the signal red? Well, I have to stop, obviously. But I'll ask David to go and use the emergency telephone so we can find out what's happening.'

2 Here are two reports about the arrests of Oswald and Ponzi.
Complete the reports with the words below.

after, arrested, drove, exactly, found, investors, president,
promised, questioning, ran, refused, shot, stopped, thousands,
wrong

John F. Kennedy was _____ as his car _____ past the Texas
Book Depository. Not long _____ the shooting, a policeman,
J. D. Tippit, _____ a man on the street. The man shot the
policeman and _____ away. Later, Lee Harvey Oswald was
_____ for murdering Tippit. Then a gun belonging to Oswald
was _____ in the Texas Book Depository, and Oswald was
arrested again – this time for killing the _____.

The well-known businessman Charles Ponzi was arrested in
Boston today. Police went to the office of Ponzi's business, the
Securities Exchange Company, which has been taking _____
of dollars a day from excited _____, and took him away for
_____. After the arrest a number of investors said that they
_____ to believe that Ponzi had done anything _____. 'He
paid me _____ what he _____,' said one, 'so I invested it all
again. He will take care of us, I'm sure.'

3 Here are newspaper headlines for some of the crimes in the
book. Which headlines go with which crimes? Which do you
prefer, and why? Write headlines for the other crimes.

DINGO KILLER – OR MURDERING MOTHER?
LAST RIDE IN A STOLEN V-8
TERRORIST – OR TERRIFIED?
MILLIONAIRE'S MONEY FOUND AT CARPENTER'S HOME
WILL WE EVER SEE HER SMILE AGAIN?

4 Perhaps lawyers said these things at the trials of some of the people in the book. Who are they talking about? Write some arguments (for and against) that lawyers could use in some of the other trials.

For: 'He is a young man who made a simple mistake. It was the bank's fault – why didn't they check his work?'
Against: 'This was a terrible crime. He was only interested in money. Because of him, a lot of people have lost their jobs!'

For: 'She hates violence. But she knew that the terrorists would kill her if she didn't do what they wanted.'
Against: 'She knew what she was doing! She robbed the bank because she wanted to help the terrorists!'

5 Do you agree or disagree with these sentences? Why?

1 If kidnappers take a child and ask for money, they should be given what they want so that the child is safe.
2 It's wrong for criminals to make money by writing a book about their crimes, even when they are out of prison.
3 If a robber comes into your house, the law should allow you to hurt or even kill them.
4 If you paint as well as Picasso, it is not a crime to sell your fake paintings for the same price as real ones.

6 Make a list of three crimes that have been in the news recently. Find out more about them, and ask some people what they think. Write a report about them.

Use these questions to help you:
 – What happened, and what was the evidence?
 – Have the police arrested anyone? Has there been a trial?
Which of the three is the most serious, and why?

ABOUT THE AUTHOR

John Escott worked in business before becoming a writer. Since then he has written many books for readers of all ages. He was born in Somerset, in the west of England, but now lives in Bournemouth in the south. When he is not working, he likes looking for long-forgotten books in small backstreet bookshops, watching old Hollywood films, and walking for miles along empty beaches.

He has written or retold more than twenty stories for Oxford Bookworms, from Starter to Stage 6, and he has also written for the Oxford Dominoes series. He has been interested in crime – both fiction and real life – since the age of thirteen, when he read a novel by the famous crime writer Agatha Christie. Many of his stories feature crime in some form, such as the adapted collection *As the Inspector Said and Other Stories* (Stage 3), and his own collection *Sister Love and Other Crime Stories* (Stage 1) which was written especially for the Oxford Bookworms Library. And Agatha Christie herself is the subject of another of his Bookworms titles, *Agatha Christie, Woman of Mystery* (Stage 3).

His other Oxford Bookworms titles at Stage 4 are *Black Beauty* (Human Interest), *The Eagle of the Ninth* (Thriller and Adventure), *Little Women* (Human Interest), *A Morbid Taste for Bones* (Crime and Mystery), *The Scarlet Letter* (Classics), *The Silver Sword* (Thriller and Adventure), and *Treasure Island* (Thriller and Adventure).

OXFORD BOOKWORMS LIBRARY

Classics • Crime & Mystery • Factfiles • Fantasy & Horror
Human Interest • Playscripts • Thriller & Adventure
True Stories • World Stories

The OXFORD BOOKWORMS LIBRARY provides enjoyable reading in English, with a wide range of classic and modern fiction, non-fiction, and plays. It includes original and adapted texts in seven carefully graded language stages, which take learners from beginner to advanced level. An overview is given on the next pages.

All Stage 1 titles are available as audio recordings, as well as over eighty other titles from Starter to Stage 6. All Starters and many titles at Stages 1 to 4 are specially recommended for younger learners. Every Bookworm is illustrated, and Starters and Factfiles have full-colour illustrations.

The OXFORD BOOKWORMS LIBRARY also offers extensive support. Each book contains an introduction to the story, notes about the author, a glossary, and activities. Additional resources include tests and worksheets, and answers for these and for the activities in the books. There is advice on running a class library, using audio recordings, and the many ways of using Oxford Bookworms in reading programmes. Resource materials are available on the website <www.oup.com/elt/gradedreaders>.

The *Oxford Bookworms Collection* is a series for advanced learners. It consists of volumes of short stories by well-known authors, both classic and modern. Texts are not abridged or adapted in any way, but carefully selected to be accessible to the advanced student.

You can find details and a full list of titles in the *Oxford Bookworms Library Catalogue* and *Oxford English Language Teaching Catalogues*, and on the website <www.oup.com/elt/gradedreaders>.

THE OXFORD BOOKWORMS LIBRARY
GRADING AND SAMPLE EXTRACTS

STARTER • 250 HEADWORDS

present simple – present continuous – imperative –
can/cannot, must – *going to* (future) – simple gerunds …

Her phone is ringing – but where is it?

Sally gets out of bed and looks in her bag. No phone. She looks under the bed. No phone. Then she looks behind the door. There is her phone. Sally picks up her phone and answers it. ***Sally's Phone***

STAGE 1 • 400 HEADWORDS

… past simple – coordination with *and, but, or* –
subordination with *before, after, when, because, so* …

I knew him in Persia. He was a famous builder and I worked with him there. For a time I was his friend, but not for long. When he came to Paris, I came after him – I wanted to watch him. He was a very clever, very dangerous man. ***The Phantom of the Opera***

STAGE 2 • 700 HEADWORDS

… present perfect – *will* (future) – *(don't) have to, must not, could* – comparison of adjectives – simple *if* clauses – past continuous – tag questions – *ask/tell* + infinitive …

While I was writing these words in my diary, I decided what to do. I must try to escape. I shall try to get down the wall outside. The window is high above the ground, but I have to try. I shall take some of the gold with me – if I escape, perhaps it will be helpful later. ***Dracula***

STAGE 3 • 1000 HEADWORDS

… should, may – present perfect continuous – *used to* – past perfect
– causative – relative clauses – indirect statements …

Of course, it was most important that no one should see
Colin, Mary, or Dickon entering the secret garden. So Colin
gave orders to the gardeners that they must all keep away
from that part of the garden in future. *The Secret Garden*

STAGE 4 • 1400 HEADWORDS

… past perfect continuous – passive (simple forms) –
would conditional clauses – indirect questions –
relatives with *where/when* – gerunds after prepositions/phrases …

I was glad. Now Hyde could not show his face to the world
again. If he did, every honest man in London would be proud
to report him to the police. *Dr Jekyll and Mr Hyde*

STAGE 5 • 1800 HEADWORDS

… future continuous – future perfect –
passive (modals, continuous forms) –
would have conditional clauses – modals + perfect infinitive …

If he had spoken Estella's name, I would have hit him. I was so
angry with him, and so depressed about my future, that I could
not eat the breakfast. Instead I went straight to the old house.
Great Expectations

STAGE 6 • 2500 HEADWORDS

… passive (infinitives, gerunds) – advanced modal meanings –
clauses of concession, condition

When I stepped up to the piano, I was confident. It was as if I
knew that the prodigy side of me really did exist. And when I
started to play, I was so caught up in how lovely I looked that
I didn't worry how I would sound. *The Joy Luck Club*

BOOKWORMS · FACTFILES · STAGE 4

Disaster!

MARY McINTOSH

From out of the sky, from under the earth, from far out at sea – disaster comes. We build, invent, and try extraordinary new things – and sometimes we bring disaster on ourselves. Today television and the Internet mean that we can watch disasters almost as they happen, and see their terrible results.

From Pompeii to the Asian tsunami, from the Great Fire of London to Chernobyl, the stories of disasters are frightening, but they have much to tell us. In this book you will find stories of fear, pain, loss, and death – but also of people whose extraordinary bravery and feeling for others will touch your heart.

BOOKWORMS · FACTFILES · STAGE 4

Nelson Mandela

ROWENA AKINYEMI

In 1918 in the peaceful province of Transkei, South Africa, the Mandela family gave their new baby son the name Rolihlahla – 'troublemaker'. But the young boy's early years were happy ones, and he grew up to be a good student and an enthusiastic sportsman.

Who could imagine then what was waiting for Nelson Mandela – the tireless struggle for human rights, the long years in prison, the happiness and sadness of family life, and one day the title of President of South Africa? This is the story of an extraordinary man, recognized today as one of the world's great leaders, whose long walk to freedom brought new hope to a troubled nation.